The Five Legs of the Cat

The Five Legs of the Cat
© 2021 Samiri Hernández Hiraldo

Saddle Road Press
Ithaca, New York
saddleroadpress.com

All rights reserved. No part of this book may be reproduced or transmitted in any form or by any means without written permission of the author.

Designed by Don Mitchell

Cover art: "Animales Sueltos" by Andrés Tavárez
andrestavarez.com

Author photograph by Adriana Fortier

ISBN 978-1-7329521-9-5
Library of Congress Control Number 2021933316

Books by Samiri Hernández Hiraldo

Black Puerto Rican Identity and Religious Experience
Al Vapor
Cuando el líquido es sólido

v 1.03

The Five Legs of the Cat

Samiri Hernández Hiraldo

Saddle Road Press

INTRODUCTION

In Puerto Rico there is the common idiom, "She is always looking for the five legs of the cat." It is said when someone is believed to try to complicate matters by overlooking and overanalyzing the situation. It assumes that this will lead to feeling overwhelmed, distressed, while causing conflict and chaos. It can also be said in a funny way while adding a sarcastic compliment of being ingenious and creative. However, more often it is meant as a critique, even a severe one. Through poetry, this book embraces the challenge of accepting some of the idiom's veracity, while leaving it up to the readers to come to their own conclusion.

This book is dedicated to those who at least open five of its pages.

Contents

Introduction — 5

First

What I Got in the Third Grade for Finishing My Math Work Early and Raising My Hand	12
Possessions	13
Tripled Persuasion	14
The Costumed Monster	15
(I Should've Known Better) God Knows Best	16
In Our Own Image	18
What Can Get Attached to Us by Default	19
Papi's Provisions	20
Prayer in Reverse	21
Primary Colors	22
The Body's Four Parts, One Quarter/a Leg Haitian	23

An Extra Paw From The First Leg

Skinprints	26
Inside Story	27
More to Do with My Mother	29
A Type of Cinderella Draft	31
Women of Intentions & Miracles	32
I've seen Demiurge's Demons…	33
Stepping Down	34
One Thing We Can Do Better	35
When Stretching Really Means Shrinking	36
Circus Operandi	37

Second

Resurrecciones de pie/Resurrections on the Feet…	40
Open Nature	42
One Land's Suffering	46
Strategies of Assisted Living	47
Under an Enclosed Bridge Before Its Grand Opening	48
More or Less to Add…	49
…The—N—word	50
Shenandoah National Park: Final Report	51
Imitations	52
Who Says the Feet Can't Stand the Snow?	54
DPTD is for Darwin's Post-Traumatic Dream	62
We Must Try Something Different	64

Third

Non-Patented	66
Second Coming	67
Gravitas/Gravités	68
Back to the Future	69
Up to the Head	70
The Ways of the Feet	71
Protagonism	73
Over Imposed	74
Nonsynonymous	75
Evolution	76
Of Legs & Gods (or The Bloody Prayer with Question Marks)	77
Backward Magic	79
Closed Up	80
Feet Apparitions	81

Fourth

Mortals	84
Alicia's Dreaming	85
Readers of a Kind	86

THE ILLUSTRATED POEM (OR MY UNCLE ON HIS VISIONARY DECEASED FATHER)	87
ALL OF US AT SOME CRISS-CROSS	88
WHO CARES FOR FIRST WHEN THERE'S SECOND (A POEM: A REINCARNATION)	89

SUCH A NAIL

WINGED	92
REPRESENTATIVE DANCER	93
MINIATURE ARTS	95
[PALIMPSEST]	96
COMORTALES	99
ART UNPARALLELED	100
gROWN IN tranSLATION	101
DOUBLED OUT	102
UP TO THE REST OF THE BODY	104
ON FEET AND MATHEMATICS	105
INVENTORS	106
THE NON-HYSTERICAL GIRL WHO CRIED OTHER THAN WOLF	108
GRACE	109
PLAYGROUNDS	110

FIFTH

PREMONITION	112
ORACLE MOMENT	113
WIDER WEB	115
WHAT WE CALL WE CALL	116
TRANSFIGURATION	117
RAIN OF FEET	118
TO PUSH FORWARD, TO GO BACK	120
OPEN-ENDED	122
THE FEET THAT BREATHE	123
ACKNOWLEDGMENTS	125
ABOUT THE AUTHOR	127

First

Which afforded leg would not possess a space?

What I Got in the Third Grade for Finishing My Math Work Early and Raising My Hand

to be able to help Doña Lydia, our janitor, and unexpectedly her daughter, and baby granddaughter

Setting the scene deliberately
in the janitor's dark closet,
rearranging 1) industrial brooms +
2) mops + 3) detergents + 4a) plastic + 4b) metal buckets=

The tender satiating and yet eager sound
as if from a new innocent species
because more & more *madres* now
away from home, sewing panties & bras in *fábricas*
with the big tap-tap of *el progreso*,

the pat-pat of *planificación familiar*. Liquified clouds
their original matte-white color
through a close-to-exploding pair of *mameyes*
(me wishing, also through my two unbloomed violets). A sudden...

oh, such marvelous sprinkle of bright yellow butterflies
spiraling on humid & sweaty grace, even though I stand,
my weak left foot keeps the heavy wooden door one fifth open

allowing inside
only

    a few sun's threads[9]

Possessions

Where have hills, creeks, falls
Big & small gone?
Who's the one responsible?
The bulldozers
To make terraplenes
For our new cement homes
To be safer, to move along with modernity, el progreso?
What have the terraplenes really given or taken?

down the eroding hill
behind my new cement house
me about seven years-old, maybe six
spotted first one leg
the rest of her body (not a Mattel) caked with dirt
most of which I immediately removed
from her matted hair, her pale face
with a spit of saliva over my flowered shirt
I said: "hola [low pitch] hola [higher pitch],"
gently shook her head
to hear the rattle of her eyes
now crossed, barely any eyelashes left
I couldn't recall if she'd been mine
Papi & Mami neither
I tried to remember until I got tired (forgot or didn't care)
I'd accepted my doll who I bathed with Vel, named "Lolin"
without one leg; my mind quite imperfect
And for days to come I played with mine,
somebody else's, mine, somebody else's, mine, somebody else's,
mine, somebody else's, mine, somebody else's doll *felizmente*

Tripled Persuasion

"When we were children, we thought and reasoned as children do. But when we grew up, we quit our childish ways." 1 Cor. 13:11.

"We have to keep bending our knees until they hurt." Once a common saying in church.

"If you have ears, pay attention." Matthew 13:9.

When I was about two or three
Mami allowed me to walk in the front yard
only in my panties with the nicest trimming
& designs despite her obsessive sense of *decencia*.
She said: "Oh, but you are my doll, *mi muñeca*."

A close relative bought my cousins and me a Barbie.
Theirs bent at the knee/Mine didn't.

Teresa, a neighbor who took care of me
gave me and her daughter (Me first 'cause I was the oldest)
an identical toy-telephone,
except for the color; she let us choose between blue and yellow
(thank God, no pink!).
I tried to forget the second:
The silence of mine and my barbie's legs.
I tried to pass along the first with the third:
The not so secret message of the telephone.
I've been more successful the fourth, the fifth time around.

The Costumed Monster

You have to call things by their name.

Not even a glimpse at first,
except for those shiny yellow rubber boots,
me swinging over sparks of *morivivi* plants
over the spiky grass in a dancing *ceremonia*.

The rest of the body is still out of sight.
But I heard his voice
thick, fat, baritone,
like the trunk of a lonely leafless palm tree offshore

followed with the wind by its own reattached echo
piercing the inanimate dark.
I couldn't believe it was Satan.
He wasn't Juan Bobo,

so stupid to let himself be recognized
not even one step at a time. Anyway I ran fast.
Next morning two thirds less afraid,
I saw the exact style of boots still wet,

painted black, grass-stained
on the first step of my uncle's front porch
behind frisky ferns and timid gardenias.
I couldn't help it.
I whispered to God
now almost empty of dread, *miedo*:

"He must be half smart, half donkey."

Much dumber than me, though.

(I Should've Known Better) God Knows Best

To el cojo of my barrio, who wore a platform shoe to compensate for his short leg, even though it didn't prevent him from limping.

To Martina at the downtown hospital, who over the years patiently performed several electrocardiograms after my babyish insistence on having a heart problem.

A little after the beginning of pubic hair, a few pimples,
a hint of Avon blue eyeliner and cherry lip gloss,
I was called to the altar for a healing miracle,
my face a pot with noodle soup over the hot stove,
to get rid of an insidious headache,
"a heart problem, a bad tumor,"
I couldn't help thinking, even though
Dr. Ramírez from the pediatric unit had confirmed
after an electrocardiogram and a prick,
it was low iron, low hemoglobin.
But Pastor Aurelio González
from the sister Candelaria Baptist Church
in the name of *el médico por excelencia*
healed my legs instead, more so the left one
making them perfectly even,
which he tested over a cold metal chair
by pulling & pushing like a stick-shift car.
I'd never realized my legs weren't of equal length.
I completely forgot about my painful cavities, my headache.

I was consumed by the pain in my right arm,
which, *pobrecita*, poor thing, had to hold my skirt & underskirt
in an almost twisted position
during such a prolonged, *transparente* miracle.

There was a popular joke about a "sambo," a man whose legs are turned inside, and goes to famous Puerto Rican televangelist, Yiye Ávila, to be healed of his problem. During the miracle the man had to ask Yiye to stop praying when his legs started to turn too much the other way. Tooth filling was another common miracle performed by Yiye Ávila.

In Our Own Image

I must've been quite asleep
to not notice Jesus coming in.
I'd left the defective screen door a little open, not thinking
of the lizards, *caculos*, ambling cockroaches,
squadrons of mosquitoes entering
regardless of Mami's tenacious spraying of the *fli*.

There's much talk about this visit I foolishly missed.
I wanted to confirm with him personally.
But he must've gone to sleep
after waiting & waiting for a smart, alert me
who could confess the one responsible
for the awful smell during last Sunday's sermon.

That it could be Machulo Pérez' languid cows
or José Rivera's precocious horses
became our first choices.
The idea that it could be one of us
seated comfortably, this time in the front row,
very unlike an Easter, a Church's Anniversary,
a Thanksgiving or Christmas visitor.

Possessed by such grimaces
we discretely checked our behinds,
definitively under our shoes while trying to keep up
with the finger-pointing message.

We knew that the one responsible
was better off leaving at the spot
'cause the smell of shit was too strong even for *el espíritu santo*.
Some of us laughed after the service was over,
our legs stomping on the floor
who knows for how many days how many times

What Can Get Attached to Us by Default

To my first-grade teacher who always let me know how much she loved me and from whom I learned how ready the mind can be to fool itself. I was still very young when she took her own life with a gun that she'd kept in her drawer.

One day going up the escalator
of the new Plaza Las Américas Mall
I thought it would become your special sleigh or float
because of your house,
your car, your jewelry, your clothes.

After years having passed
I went up the escalator of old Plaza Carolina
barefoot
looking like the hippie students of *la universidad*,
independentistas, sellers of Krishna food

at the sound of folk *nueva trova*.
I'd almost become another persona.
Going down my feet underneath with a texture of straight lines,
the lines moving in different directions, intertwined.
The soles got reattached.

Papi's Provisions

For once I heard you sobbing
at the thickest edge of *la loma*
behind our newly rebuilt cement home still with bare blocks
dancing showing off their bottoms,
behind your workshop with many holes
because of time, heat, humidity, hurricanes.

Almost lost in the gripping thick grass, smelling turpentine,
I felt your tears go astray before managing over vines of *grosellas*
while I stood on top of a pigmented rock half-subterranean
trying on my two feet moving right to left, right to left
to keep my mature deep-breathing, red velvety balance.

It took me a while coming back to a you and a me to the us,
you laying it on my aluminum plate once again
a single green banana
cause you had to sell each & every one of the others,
yellow, purple, blue, orange.

Prayer in Reverse

But her. Amen.
the cancer delivered, burnt, or evaporated.
on a slanted, falling apart stove could make
Not even a ripped sandal false step
now for the filled hot *caldero* to finally spill.

her hands glued to her improvised apron,
She waited & waited,
cilantro, oregano, and sweet peppers.
with a mix of olive oil, garlic,

her neck, her shoulders, her arms & legs
speaking in tongues after anointing her head,
switching to the simple lyrics of a *corito*,
singing three verses of an old hymn,
she didn't ask right then, but declared herself healed
on a premature morning,
Peeling bianatos, yuccas, malangas, and plantains

each sunray a branch ready to nest a miracle.
spooning one sunray at a time through the only window,
I got my last impression of Eudocia Benítez
I have to say it was in her humble kitchen

Primary Colors

That's something else I learned, don't remember where and when first, that red is considered king of all colors, including by the Zapotecs.

Ear shooting the animistic bleached water
My eyes sketched you blue-swimming
Absorbed by the undertaking of your determined legs
Closing my eyes I dreamed I loved you in vibrant red
(exactly the way you have wanted)
It happened on an early steamy morning
Announced by colloquial birds in such a unique timbre
Before the humming of what seemed translucent archangels
Your left hand touched the plain cement first
Your feet, toes wrinkled, barely second, third. Then,
Most notoriously, you made a close U turn
While I was taking my time to a clotted silence,
Getting more & more wet, almost completely drenched
To a determined you
Now coming out of the most efficient dryer
Wearing your scuffed heavy boots
You kept your distance (didn't offer a towel)
Staring at the tic toc high above
Oozing an audible posterior siren
For what seems beyond the annual curfew
Some self-imposed definite deadline
There were coagulated leaves
From the few trees left, almost making it in the half-empty parking area
I looked slowly drying, dripping less & less, for a fermented sign
Inside an empty plastic container
Inside a torn plastic bag
Between hot, fading yellow lines

The Body's Four Parts, One Quarter/a Leg Haitian

"The Dominican Republic deported an estimated 70,000 to 80,000 people of Haitian descent over three years. Those left behind live in a state of institutionalized terror." –Jonathan M. Katz, November 12, 2018, The Atlantic.

I knew the almost perfect couple
/*Conocí a la pareja casi perfecta*
He the period, she "right before the next sentence"
/*Él por ser punto, ella aparte*
One or two spaces in between
/*Uno o dos espacios de por medio*
She a Dominican and he a Puerto Rican
/*Ella dominicana y él puertorriqueño*

Their children *un cuarto haitianos*
/a quarter Haitian
Ellipsis_____

An Extra Paw From The First Leg

What is a tail isn't just a black or white tail.

Skinprints

Still my footprints next to those of our hens
on the defective cement sidewalk
beside my grandmother's house in my old *vecindario* of Puerto Rico.

I wonder where they would've gone
if they'd been left up in the squishy mud
with footprints of our biggest pig or goat.

Would Mami and Papi look alike
if after their many steps holding hands going to Río Piedras,
they had not given birth to my brother & me?

There's much to absorb by the pathways molded by dissimilar feet
stepping on & out the hard dirt,
the germinated flaky green almost one with the bluest air,

to be regaled immersed in the gripping valley
filled with breathings, skin oils, steps,
coming downs, going ups, East or West.

My overly attached handprints to such bewildering soils—
Papi & Mami over my permeable skin
more than a passing memory.

Inside Story

For my father who became as good at sharing the bread of life as at climbing trees barefoot to get fruits for anyone who came by or not, and for my mother who apparently stared at him like a mere statue.

It could have been the sequential nights,
he the child resting his premature legs,
feet on the wall, paint peeling off with a map of Earth.
Lying down, drinking milk from his special bottle,
the sound apparently bothered his sister Gisela
whom he's attached to more than his mother.

The child becomes slowly but surely no longer a child,
the good soil, the big tree,
the leading star you could count on.
Busier than ever at thirty-three
he gives the perfect response, personal,
mailed to you as a small piece
of paper inside tinted glass for free—
a positive solution for life's troubles,
a formula for good things to continue uncoiling.

The man is proud to be the only son,
his dad the most successful electrician
who opens in less than three days the most rapturous dark;
a conductor of anticipated red energy in someone's path,
anyone willing to grab their life

by their feet: *Shouldn't it take some pause,
that type of unforeseen, perhaps odd twisting?*

"One of the most life-determining exercises,"
the son clarifies in a TED talk
surrounded by all sorts of people
with a range of random possibilities; the son
in his electrical wheelchair. But life is still fair,

sometimes, maybe most of the time
if you learn to sacrifice, to grab in another way, *de otra manera*;
(unlike his sister Gisela)?

Is the man the jungle kid from TV
who once grabbed with his feet after Tarzan,
Tarzan who grabbed with his feet after Cheetah,
Cheetah most probably after God.
God who does and is everything, The Verb,
way long before The Word,
through big and small vowels glued to consonants,
assisting himself in revealing things to us *en carne y hueso*,
such minuscule details like the difference
between "i" and "y," as in "business" and "busyness"?

Un extranjero preacher at my humble childhood church
in the Barrazas' mountains once referred to us
no matter who we are, how we look, where we've come from,
as God's Business, turning god automatically
into the buttoned-up CEO Jesus of painter Clifford Davis,
a briefcase in his left hand, busy grabbing us.

I'm still not sure after all.
I keep turning around, seeing another child
like those once on the screen during Missionary Week,
in the newspaper, the doctor's office magazine,
on big and small screens.
I try in silence to decipher the silent "e,"
the child's neck, hands and feet,
dirty nails, sunken eyes on an earthen floor,
gasping for the ample breeze.
"There's Gisela!," someone announces.
She's carrying the child like she's done her brother all her life.

More to Do with My Mother

I

I heard the biggest balloon almost pop
Grandfather and Uncle fighting drunkenly of course
Mami trying to prevent another family *tragedia*
Me screaming, opening & closing my frantic eyes
Mami trying to get the *machete* off their possessed hands
I saw her fingers coated with blood,
Then myself blowing such fire on my grandfather's and my uncle's toes
Happy Birthday Forgiveness! It is now as it was before
The balloon kept growing — Mami in my chest a miraculous size

II

Mami and I conversed a few times
propping ourselves up with our elbows moisturized
with a mix of Jergens and Cocoa Butter
closer to the edge of her full-size bed
with posts almost poking through the roof, about the difference
between she already a woman and me not-yet
or to-become. She trying my translucent pantyhose,
the pantyhose not reaching where it is supposed to.
Me walking on her color taupe, a little bent,
working extras under each foot and around my petite waist.
Little pressure between my legs.

III

As far as I remember I've been sitting on
my dark green rocking chair
head back, feet up, since I finally stop
demanding Mami
to keep her toenails completely polished or unpolished and short,

to wear belts that match her outfits,
right at her belly button, not higher or below,

and to avoid hairspray
on her unrelaxed, dirty hair
to prevent it from looking porous;
from smelling like a wet scary cat or a dry miserable dog.

A Type of Cinderella Draft

IA.

My first experience with *liberación*
happened at my Baptist church
located in my father's "white" *barrio*,
a Sunday a little after 11 a.m.
at the skirt of the recently refurbished altar
aproned with roses, lilies and carnations,
during an evangelistic campaign
(coinciding with the revival week of the Pentecostal Iglesia Bethania).

IB.

Such *liberación* was performed
by a Pentecostal guest male preacher
on a dark-skinned thirteen-year old girl named Virgen
with *pelo malo* ("bad" or kinky hair).
She always sat in the back pews,
like most members of my church's mission
located in my mother's "superstitious" "black" *barrio*.

II

I heard her scream and scream, her hair getting messier and messier.
Like a witch? I saw her. Running away.
Leaving behind at least her left

III

leather sandal. "In a Dream: I wished…"

VI

But oh, how many times I've imagined myself trying to fit even my
right foot in

V

her sandal. And I write about it —My foot not fitting.

Women of Intentions & Miracles

I. Why it changed to a white tunic, and over long pants mainly
There was a time when baptism by immersion
semi-dressed Baptist women of tampering sin
(as if for the first time publicly)
> The spiritual undress has now transferred
> from the perimeter of the women's shivering hands
> trying to keep their slips, dresses, skirts down
> to avoid showing above their knees
> and in between,
> while the frigid water
> keeps trying to lift the slips, the dresses, the skirts
> from the bottom like red umbrellas

The same women began wearing their thickest brassieres
among waves & waves & waves of adjustments

II. Why it didn't stay the same way from nakedness
(first step with the left)
Young Neida of no tampons
collected between her legs, piles of semi-Augusts
> water on the road ready to perform, "Eucalyptus"

Middle-age Neida of Kotex
legs side by side any week's Saturday through Monday
> overall skin, linen for any necessary Ms. Absorbing

(second step also with the left)
Neida's no-pads, no-tampons
half-stored, no clothes not just on the twenty-fours
unshelved most days of any check-marked or not season
vines wrapping around—a tested vessel of Lord Jesus

I've seen Demiurge's Demons...

searching for dazzling Lesotho diamonds
camouflaging their real name
(subbing the "e" with an "ia," adding a second "d" almost at the end).

But I've mostly seen them every time I've almost completely craned
and twisted my already bristled neck with syndrome.
Thank goodness I've never been an occasion ring, a necklace,
nor have I turned into a pillar of salt
or an old Jamaican plantation sugarcane.

> "But his wife, from behind him, looked back, and she became a pillar of salt." Genesis 19:26.

Stepping Down

i wish i would've gotten off the gloss pews more often walked down the tiled stairs over the half-gravel-half-asphalt parking lot even if i had damaged my mother's new violet high heels which she let me wear after my babyish insisting gone through the smoke of small and boat-size cars passing by on one and a half lane curves took off my shoes over the unpaved slanted sidewalk covered by tall and trimmed grass even if my feet got hurt by rocks pointy sticks crushed beer bottles burned by lit cigarette buds caked by stinky mud dog cow or horse manure made it to my maternal grandparents' home to wash their dirt crusted feet their soles engraved with cuts even if it meant not singing hymns with my father's side back in the choir in perfect harmony

One Thing We Can Do Better

In English: "Yet you have made them a little lower than God..." 1 Co. 8:5
In Spanish: "Le has hecho poco menor que los ángeles
[You have made him less than the angels]"
"Neither animals nor angels know redemption." The words of a preacher back in
Puerto Rico whose name I can't remember.

Holes from cows' hooves
in *la loma* further down
caused my cousins & me to trip,
especially when we sprinted.
Oh, how we wished
we were *puros perros y perras*,
simple male and female dogs.
Although all that tripping might have made our feet & ankles
half-uneasy, half-strong.
Eventually we stopped.

When Stretching Really Means Shrinking

And hasn't my luck always been a shadow
Stepping out, stretching? –David Rivard

One jumped
in the backyard of my suburban subdivision 4bd/2bth home.
Five years later another tried to cross
right in front of me driving in a rush my dark green 2004 Honda
Accord
(recently recalled) on my way to Shell Point.
I saw him. Dead. I turned into his shadow.
Days had to follow.
I realized I jumped like him
in my own backyard after my very own shadow.
Then I remembered he hadn't even crossed.
He was as scared as I was on the side of Wakulla Arran Road.
The deer.
Oh my dear was still breathing alive
like I was:
He, mostly between St Joe's tall skinny pine trees;
me, mostly between Heritage Turner's prefab drywalls.
I recently moved to the woods like those in Puerto Rico.
Not sure if all of my shadows their shades rockabyed.

Circus Operandi

My mother and I watched on TV a young woman who did most of everything with her legs. "But she lost both arms," my mother had to clarify a few times, me rolling my eyes.

We dust off our extra-velvety Kung Fu shoes
next to a broken and cold body.
Pull back from "next in line" onto such a tightrope walking
exposing the trembling mostly from our hips up.

It is without a doubt the persistent drama of "back-and-forth"
between our anchoring and our loosening up,
more exhausting than between thoughts of Iguazu Falls
and "Julia de Burgos' river" reflections.

We occupy ourselves with The Absurd
changing of the whole deal in a single snap,
in a flash
resting on the safest, the most stable flat.

The Absurd quite personified comes a second time
dressed as a colorful super funny clown,
rides in circles on a rattling funky bike, honking the horn.
Turns into a black-and-white *personaje mágico*, yellow wings attached,
makes us all his "magnifique!" assistants
stand up from our newly designed, padded orange seats,
roll over the ground covered by purple curtains
to a drawing of the highest blue-and-white hills.
Lying down we clap with our grey-coated bare feet,
rope after rope hanging from our blind backs.
We could turn once more vertical.

Second

A wounded deer leaps highest.
　　—Emily Dickinson

Resurrecciones de pie/Resurrections on the Feet...

No es que a la muerte le haya dado con caminar detrás nuestro casi pisándonos los talones, sacándonos la sandalia para llamar la atención nada más.

con marca y todo
Después de su ultraje y mutilación
creí que Dios iba a aplastarnos a todas y a todos
de una vez, presionando tan y tan fuerte,
que hasta íbamos a derretirnos y a desaparecer
mucho antes de todo su pie tocar finalmente.

Pero no creo estar segura
de que haya completamente pasado—
Algunos de nosotros surgiendo como lodo bastante mojado
alrededor del pie, bordeando entre los dedos,
por el hueco seco que dejó el mohoso clavo.

(with mark and everything
After her rape and mutilation
I thought God was going to step on all of us
at once pressing very very hard,
that we would melt and disappear
even before his foot could fully come down.

I'm not sure he has done it yet—
Some of us coming as sloppy mud
around his foot's edges, between his toes,
through the dry hole made by the rusted nail.)

—

pasado el rosario mayormente de mujeres
Frotando los dedos de los pies
de uno a uno, de cinco en cinco, de diez en diez,
de un grupo al otro, de uno al otro
se olvidan de por medio los espacios.

(*after the rosary mainly by women*
Rubbing the toes
one by one, five by five, ten by ten

from one group to another, from one to the other
the space in between is almost forgotten.)

—

de hueso remojado
Una madre que encuentra uno de los huesos muertos,
por ejemplo, el de la pierna de un hijo en el desierto,
le pega plumas completamente abiertas,
por secar, por volar — Ha de ser su mayor aplicadora.

(*of rewetted bone*
A mother who finds one of the dead bones,
for example, of a son's leg in the desert,
glue bird feathers completely open,
ready to dry, to fly — Must be its best applicant.)

—

contrario al reloj
La niña yanomamo
que repartiendo flores en vez de arroz
a cambio de agua limpia
de cabeza al suelo,
sus piernas sin salirle alambres de oro
quince para el cielo

(*contrary to the clock*
The Yanomamo girl
distributing flowers instead of rice,
in exchange of clean water
her head to the ground,
the legs without gold wires coming out
marking fifteen 'til heaven)

Open Nature

Younger sister Lynette
must have footprints on the palms of her hands.
Older brother Luis Enrique,
alias Raquel, who usually complains & complains
seems to have lately decided
to follow the steps of Lynette
who lost both legs at an early age.

Raquel now complains less & less
right, left;
anywhere in the middle.

—

She's a type of psychic who reads underneath the shoes,
who doesn't look for the obvious, the less obvious, the anticipated or
the overdue,
but for the completely faded over unattainable surfaces.
Having been trained walking barefoot, naked; no food but pain
in the smoky dark, waiting to die, finally dead
in a secret not so secret location in Poland...

—

played the game, of the crocodile?
facing up/soft
facing down/hard
forced in either case to open the legs
until such painful wider than usual,
unlike the almost closing prison bars,
for sure & regardless of such layer
of neon blue on the overcoated walls,
as if the much-activated relaxed sky;
the persistent, desperate shaking
always in the dim background
of breathing/breaking tail — ¡Pura Libertad!

—

A poplar grew next to his home
He always assumed he was too small, too short
He clambered to see Jesus (like long time not up)
He straddled branch after branch
But no multitude, no Jesus
Not even a tiny depiction
The rest of his life he waited for Yaupon Holly
To grow out of a goat's skin or papyrus

—

They say you must live one day at a time,
one day at a time, oh one day at a time
tossing some weight behind, some way,
someday behind each step. We say you learn
about time if we get to cry; I cry you cry
Stepping aside. Clearing our tears.
A foot, an inch, a centimeter at a time?
I never gotten happy going down a Barrazas' cliff on a junky bike,
the legs as if *cada una por su lado*, never connected.

—

When we think about a hang(wo)man
We imagine head up feet down—
The feet unbreathing, untouching the mere ground

To hang on the head or on the feet
Same human/suffering

Head, hands, and feet trying to reach simultaneously
A hanging dream?

—

Is resurrection a sign of relentlessness?
The small mouse I saw the other slithering night running from here
to there and everywhere, very fast,
while dreaming about you, suddenly stopped,
then whispered in my feverish ear a quite humid secret:
What I must do contrary to the bellowing currents of the Wakulla
River—

Quedarme quieta   still   still   still
possessing no feet/well-accepting it. But it didn't state plainly
1) for how long, 2) to which direction, 3) if compared to
Artemidorus' mummy

—

Spring has untied its laces kindly
People walking squeezing each other not exactly
Under drops of purified smells rushing over new birth surroundings
They're swathed in fortuitous hope quite astounding

Leaves & petals are engraved at & beyond the edges of sweaty & dry skins
They also cover curved lines of shoes emptied of feet, precisely

—

She's kept
a discreet profile
letting her distance
from her own liquifieds

hoping for almost
the complete opposite
focusing on her drieds
But it pours for the down-to-earth astronaut

—

Perhaps I would never visit Culebra, Uruguay, Zanzibar, Bhutan, Indonesia
Perhaps I would die as filaments spread between tender knuckles
From stuck to stuck to stuck to Unstuck to stucK
Un-paramount of an albatross
A triangle with one size
Never fully winded
Escorted in part
Half opaque
Stuttering/

                              Stepping over the next line

—

At some point
We separate or divorce from this mythic life.
Elena has insisted on the last more than twice,
That bubbling time of cursive-signing papers (long-time printed,
también acogidos oralmente).
Strings of land being deforested
Involving literal cuts.
Should we keep hiking love?

One Land's Suffering

To the many more who've passed away with a lying death certificate, or none.

Such an allergic reaction ready for its very own title,
"Sad Mixed Miracle"—
the twin towers squeezing down on September 11, 2001
like the legs of a Tutsi or Hutu child
slaughtered to scattered dust sometime during 1994

—

Many feet after being kidnapped, tortured, murdered,
thrown away to the waters, hidden under the Atacama Desert,
for the most part forgotten, ignored, except for *las madres*;
que no habrán de hacer ellas por sus hijos (what won't they do for their children).
Some have dared to classify the mothers as "stagnant"
for not stepping out of *la misma etapa* (the same phase).
But to those who've called I heard someone say:
"Perhaps you've never pierced through the clouds,
your eyes a child's tongue licking the largest unicorn lollipop
from the very bottom to the very top.
A few planets, millions of stars-añañuca flowers-loving bones."
I couldn't agree more.

Strategies of Assisted Living

To the residents of Eden Springs in Crawfordville, FL.

To greet with the backside of the head while speaking nonsense
> *Avoiding any judgment*
> *during whatever*
> *time, including eternity, it might take*
> *any indulgent closeness*

To compete with the cutting-the-edge rain through the hallway exit, going the opposite way
> *Still learning consistency*
> *and bringing awareness*
> *that the point isn't to win any race*
> *or to jump over the back or face-to-face*

To donate even the blood that microscopically sprays the air while trying to find the vein
> *Imagining the self*
> *apart & away*
> *in another reappearing body, even in a click or whistling language*
> *with its corresponding facelessness*

To eat a freckled banana, opening it from the bottom up, legs up making the letter "u" instead of the letter "i"
> *or "v"– remembering human life is,*
> *yes, indeed*
> *similar, but not the same as all the world's chimps*
> *who've made it*

Under an Enclosed Bridge Before Its Grand Opening

Halfway 2012 after Hurricane Debby
right on the Ochlockonee Bay,
Doug Harvey's accused of continuing to confuse
the roaring of trucks over the recently repaired bridge (after
Hurricane Dennis)
with the roaring of the thunder over the bay & its consequences.
"Aren't many trucks over one bridge,
many bridges under the same thunder?" asks the defense.
"How much longer?" asks the prosecutor.

Ninety-three-year-old Mrs. Betty Donaldson
from the jury immediately stands up
in the middle of a sudden, almost tactile silence, minus
the echoed click of her knees,
the subtle sound of her Depends, her black low heels.
She asks: "How long is life to compare, to confuse with?"
after years having ridden her childhood yellow bike
over a different type of bridge, pedaling & pedaling
barefoot against the massive gray sky,
drawing hundreds of daisies, their petals piercing more than the
mere ground.

More or Less to Add...

Long before AC African people did the math:
how to cool down the hot air of South Carolina? —Nikky Finney

   no more black heads attached to the rest of the exhausted
bruised stems
in the shrinking fields Those who escaped the shackles, the chains
    the ropes the blades left the south as raw cotton
    the road
Didn't simply roll down as in "just from South Carolina to Native
Florida"
    Didn't simply roll up as in "just from Alabama to Kansas to
Detroit"
Weren't simply flown away   They "added on top"
     some of the raw color of what they encountered
going step by step on The Road
    to the new promised dreamable
    Canaan Neither they turned
    into mere dirtier compressed cotton
    Nor into new dyed fabric
    propelled solely by noisy, smelly and hot
    motor

...THE—N—WORD

[Drayton Hill Plantation]
See this is them on two legs,
This higher one here-on four. —Nikky Finney

    If you push them enough with such heavy weight on top, they become more

              [The Philippines]
              NATIVES NEAR MANILA: THESE PEOPLE REPRESENT THE LOWER ORDERS AND MIXED RACES. THEIR SQUATTING POSITIONS, SIMILAR TO THE MONKEY'S FAVORITE ATTITUDE, INDICATES A NO-DISTANT REMOVAL FROM THE 'CONNECTING LINK.'
              OUR ISLANDS AND THEIR PEOPLE, 1899-George Black

    If we all push each other, heavy or not
We can restart whatNever — No soul

Shenandoah National Park: Final Report

He, a successful well-equipped hiker, hikes
On his tennis shoe, a discrete drop of sweat —
Phlegm over the barefoot of a hillbilly young girl
Who sings with such an accent about Joy & Pain,
The sign of backwardness, isolation,
Of something wrong with that tiny corner of the universe.

He reads one day by chance, after coming down breathing fast
On an archaeology journal:
"Complex Migration" (before the 1920s)
"Expulsion of Hillbillies" (during the 1920s and 1930s)
"Hippies/Folk Utopia" (1960s and 1970s)
"More Than a Family Adventure" (from the 1990s to the present)
"Archaeological Site" (up to *la memoria*).

He climbs a third, fourth time.
Observes absolutely more:
The young white girl — a teenage boy
Who reads trashed *National Geographic*,
Drinks warm fermented coke.
The son of a hard-working farmer whose skin color is purple.

The hiker hikes, settles. He hikes & settles, down & up
Up & down not only dirt layers:
progress, dream, purpose,
Stereotypes, eagerness; common sense?
Complex reality, imagination, profound research:
Substituted persistence

IMITATIONS

Not even when we genuflect can we squirt some air to be taken away.

Who would've not after knowing Pedro,
collected some of his most giving steps,
arranged them with their breathings in sequence,
put them in a tin or glass container
like *montunos, caramelos* or popcorn kernels
to be birthday or Christmas gifted or donated?

It should be the usual protocol,
but life isn't that simple.
We can't pass on body parts like infectious disease
if we want to continue being part of this world.

Many have seen thieves
digging under tissues seizing bones,
thieves perfect at tiptoeing before installing refrigerators,
even before the fridges having been in the solid imagination.

I've heard what isn't a preserved salted secret.
Pedro concluding once about nothing in particular,
me against his warm skin (not a pint of fever).
"As it is given, it's always been."
We continue to breathe in-&-out-&-out-&-in,
the summarizing symbol of phe-no-me-no-lo-gi-cal existing,
as if it was our original conceit, our initial agreement.
Some living without any specific humid, dry, hot breathing.

Can you picture them, those unlike many of us
trying to drink lemongrass tea,
the honey staying at the bottom
after much heavy stirring?

Many breathe and drink where there's nothing.
Ask a Rohingya, a Yemeni, a Syrian, a Sudanese!
We're the very humans who can share the drink
but who can't drink or even breathe
for our neighbor, close, distant.

Our arms might not be long enough for that,
our legs cut too short.
Our heart doesn't follow their path.

Who Says the Feet Can't Stand the Snow?

Who says the feet can't stand the snow?
They don't call them Christmas paperweight for nothing.
They don't.
(Who thought to knock down the greatest number of feet as in bowling below zero degree?)

Lino showed God his fist out of his left foot
Full of doubt
    Carlitos his nephew, on the other hand,
        made a for-sure baby mark
            with the outer side of his right fist on Lino's dirty car's back window
He used the tip of his fingers for the toes, while smiling right at God

Can tibias bark under the skin of domesticated owners?

Where oh steadiness your victory, between the feet and the feet*ed*?

He got tired
of her interrupting any you & me significant moment
to upload to Facebook
He paid back with photographing
his footprints
at a one-way,
not-turning-back distance

How beautiful are the feet of those who announce
the good news of the coming of the heart

A foot gets
one side of the sun at a time—
What's left (?)

O older Chinese women, you who tortured yourselves by binding your feet for long periods of time to permanently change their shape, making them small and rounded for the sake of Lotus beauty, to please men, as it was believed it would tighten the muscles of your vagina making sexual intercourse more pleasurable to them. Is there *next?*

Who's to change their dry shoes;
unlike those who change the water of their indoor cactus.

Often times, my brother & I got mad
At Papi for being barefoot most of the time
Even in the company of visitors
As if he, us, we were all poor jíbaros

But all is soon added or subtracted,
The feet, the beads in the abacus of love

There are extreme extremities
For example, feet on glasses
All on four legs

Known as "The Player Woman,"
she played all the piano keys with the feet she could—
Up the roof, an unframed mirror

A hole carved on the wall, not any wall, less of a foot of an eye

Do marks on the stomach wing after they've walked?

Such tiny feet
Such tender zigzagging
No time for no hope to imagine

One step at a time isn't only for those patient enough
        or those who   easily jump
into other than their
        handful con   ductions

Cypress, Cypress
What can we say of your raisin-like knuckles
Telling all but that which has been suppressed

The nose, the toes
Without forgetting the breasts, hard to cover—the stomach
What we eat we put inside first, twice; outside multiplied?

To become a third leg the _____ doesn't need a special coagulation

On the *Wakulla News (8/5/15)*
there was an article
about Capt. Jack finding a foot
& calf deep down
the St. Marks River
Many of us got disappointed
it wasn't a real person's
but a simple old mannequin's

That shadows aren't only stretched by the feet; this I know in an afternoon.

Don't mess with me
I have a bigger heart than my feet
Ok, go ahead, do mess
All the feet I have are too small for the heaviest burden

A step after step after step, in the same order, isn't

Feet Wallpaper

Head and shoulders knees and toes, knees and toes
80 percent of space unexplored, pain or joy, pain-joy?

There's no ladder
To patternless clouds
Sandra drew on the cement attached to the ground
Millions of eyes
There's silence now
As we pass hot death
From the hand to the leg

Park of pigeons in San Juan
Dos tipos de extensiones competitivas

Never treat legs like shovels
For less

Guare shook his boots:
    manured soil

    termite particles
    half of a toothpick
    newspaper's ashes
Then it was his feet's turn

Could a shaggy grass survive a nervous foot?
Is underneath the feet abstained from open hair, could it at least
siphon sweat, grab some breeze?

The human feet that traveled about 70,000 years ago
Out of Africa
Are/aren't of this world

"Let me borrow your legs." Once upon a time *mi tan linda abuela*.

If the tongue could walk,
would more words escape the rain even *en el mero desierto*?

A man sitting small
kept looking
at the biggest (or bigger than himself) toe, says the congregation.
He kept looking
at a big toe
away a few inches,
and at any small
across the multi mirrors covering the roof from below, adds the Lord.

Kicking the meter to gain or to reappropriate

Same bed
two pairs of legs with restless-leg syndrome
Each at their own rhythm,
except when singing publicly in unison, "A Perfect Trio"

People with elephantiasis,
Because of their head, ears, or their legs?

Abuela's hands touching hot pots
Her feet on the Lord's test of lit ashes

The Spirit keeps up with the dancing
even with the splinter on the pantyhose,
such a long thread in the panties

Those small footprints,
aquellas pequeñas huellas
on the cement.
Going back trying to fit the big ones
inside — *Para llenarse de pieles memorias.*

A painter
Painted
With her foot, much more than her mind, one can assume

Since to many of us
It's hard to imitate
The girl wearing
A watch on her ankle...

My feet climbing the rest of my body/I wait for the head

Oh, how I thought I carried soldiers right in my pocket
Until I got to listen carefully to Tío Guancho *por lo menos una noche*
Found a soldier-toy in my washer, not only his legs part of the most
common & larger green landscape

Do stars see us the way we see them—
At the same time, the corners, the feet   in different
gravitational atmospheres?

Shelling pounds and pounds of beans
Mercedes' feet took time to grow out of the shells. Her mouth
already
one with the longest branches

How many more feet can the flames in the picture turn to particles?

Metió las patas de seguro una mujer
(Let it in, it had to be a woman)."
This is to avoid mentioning the thing
belonging to the poor little man,
which enters like a beast.

orgasmic l e g   s/doubtofsilence

Any place could get the feet first
Including the doctor's office scale

Even if one foot at a time
According to vultures, the last end

One pair of feet on the sand
Of Jesus or the people—before and after the processional ritual

Kept her feet under the sofa cozy cushion
Regardless of the strong wind
Her dream with venereal repetitions

Buttoned the shirt down to the legs/There Pablito went

My grandmother's front part of her feet
Salad tongs, pliers, trash-picks
She was that kind of species

Those who lose their legs keeping themselves/Yes to them!

Bastet had two legs and she was a cat, an Egyptian cat, but a goddess cat.

One can be certain
That someone in this world
Has touched
A mummy's feet
In a day
Many inches from memory

Rain isn't gasoline under the feet. It's not. It should not

Could anyone live
stepping each moment
as unequivocally,
between the toes immortal?

Just because the feet reach the night they don't have to abbreviate or summarize

Some people, maybe poets,
are born to identify the person
on the folding that has been cut
following the lines of the original, waist down matching or not

A real mask leaves eyeholes at the feet of blue-sky — to Arnoldo
Roche Rabell

My little brother once
Thought wrinkles could transfer
From his pants to his legs
So he wore his pants on his arms,
And he walked again

Who would not love more than a foot?

Quem não tem sapatos vai a pé

El Indicativo/Mami pressing hard with her left foot sitting next to
Papi driving his green Ford truck

Juanito drew the tip of his toe touching God's
His pastor made him erase it all

Could I step in the unpredicted silence of the future?
Could silence be stepped on to be emptied, or to make noise?

Ouch is for the smallest toes. Footworks!!!

It isn't the same, it is not
a foot over a wheel from the side
as if a foot over a wheel from the very bottom

Those crossed feet elevated, sharpened like a blade with words.

Co-pilot's half-leg *de andar no cualquier aterrizaje*

Rahini polished her nails
And her girls' and their girls'
And their sisters', cousins' and neighbors' girls' and their girls' and
their girls'
And the goddess' way above & beyond the cuticles

Words coming all wet after the feet having been over puddles only a
day?

Pina dans plus d'une de ses danses
a écrit avec ses pieds
non seulement en français, ci-dessous aussi

Pina in more than one of her dances
has written with the feet
not only in French, also underneath

Are the legs of the octopus the octopus' legs?

There are the feet, the nomads' feet
That also rest on pupils

A Russian doll coming out of the other and the other and the other;
no split legs

Volatile feet/Head underneath/Non-explosive

When he left the sock hanging from the spike, the bird hadn't just started to fly

The legs of the black cats during the Black Death Plague, poor rats or poor humans?

And what have my feelings given in return
to the steps of past people?
I still can't tell who am I with & without
a type of capsule, an open-wish capsule

DPTD is for Darwin's Post-Traumatic Dream

Inspired by the documentary "Darwin's Nightmare" by Hubert Sauper.
Darwin also used the word love many times, even if he thought of his theory as devilish.

Old and young (footprints & not in the smelly, squishy mud)
eating almost exclusively whatever was left on the bones
hanging on rusty wires, the bones of the small fish
not-completely eaten yet by the big introduced to Lake Victoria to be over-caught,
exported to exclusive markets,
served over fancy tablecloths.

It is called HUMAN SURVIVAL.
This time not the Darwinian,
but the type everyone in their right or wrong mind
can easily notice. Is it that one way or another we the living stay living?

Pause—
"Darwin, o Darwin, still your fault
(and of those who came along,
like Alma Whittaker, according to Elizabeth Gilbert,
those who came before).

Your evolution (vs. creation).
Such antidote distraction from the other,
the common "what to expect(?)"
The living daily-living in different forms, different shapes.

No exceptions. Some big. Some small.
Some in betweens.
Overall
We aren't the same...we are, but we are not.
Some with two shoes.
Some with only one.
Some with half of a shoe.
Some barefoot.
Without feet altogether

(a half-nail on an imagined gigantic toe).
All our bones.
What was left inside the small fish
That's inside the largest fish that still exists.
In which flowing water? Through which mouth?
At which table? What size are the legs & the arms?
Selected loving peaks and wings
into the Tanzanian Infinite?

We Must Try Something Different

[A]nd the street of the city was pure gold... (Revelation 21:21)

Today
I want no other thing
No other thing than streets of Papua gold
Shiny, cold, refreshing
No slashed-&-burned horticultural soil
No wild grass
No bamboo floors
No Bakhtiari wool nor 100% organic cotton rugs

I want them here
Right now
For my soul
And at least, Xarl's, Amado's, Martin's, Pierre's, Nick's
Nancy's, Alexandra's, Fatima's, Mrs. Froggy's
I've wanted
Too many sustainable things
For too long

Third

What about the legs of the giraffe?

Non-Patented

> "*Over the weekend Rael and his design partner Virginia San Fratello installed their three pink seesaws along the U.S. and Mexico border, ensuring each side had a perfect balance. [C]hildren and adults were connected in meaningful ways on both sides[.]*" –Stacey Leasca, July 31, 2019, Travel + Leisure.

What else should summon us
to the art of welcoming life,
any life,
a su vez no cualquiera?

After an original dilation scene
(the next station or case #4016)
in a platform, an open earthen mold
of a pair of wide-opened legs.
Its exuded replica
on the other side of the wall,
one leg behind,
        one leg in front.

Innumerable repetit[c]ion(e)s.

Second Coming

To think like a child we must not be one.

December inflated
bit by bit
since January 31 or September 13
with accumulated Santa Claus dreams.
    It stopped such gymnastics
        of the most anticipated quite desperate, quite ambitious,
what-to-get list
    (predicting
        some slow, medium-to-hard learning).
All of a sudden,
sparkled ribbons curled into one drizzled night.
Close to its end, a pint-sized bright light.
Using the language of innocent, playful angels.
A stretched yellow balloon to a resurrected Christ.
That he had to be born first
completed the full over-the-line sentence.
An overloaded request
with luring, surprisingly mature eloquence.
Even if difficult to carry on for only a few small steps,
which already caused a group of those close to the manger,
brightened with green lights,
to make several trips back. A start.
A POP! The most exponential
keeping   less & less,
chewing,
swallowing down to cloth diapers.
Some sort of a red-stained after.
Out of the big blue piñata before its other after.

Gravitas/Gravités

Los pies también lloran (The feet also cry) after the Mexican soap opera, Los ricos también lloran (The rich cry too).

(Pain of a single, singled-out Nuyorican, *madre de crianza*, adoptive mother)
After no money to eat for over a month,
her second-hand brassiere had to withhold
more than her massive gelatinous breasts
right when she first heard how her adopted son
who dressed up like Myrta Silva/Rita Moreno en *sus comienzos*
took his/her own self
The mother's legs couldn't
the rest of her already semi-suspended body
like maples, its leaves signaling the ever-standing fall

(Pain of a mother and a father, coupled finally back on la *isla del encanto*, the island of enchantment)
Five years of daily subsistence
getting in & out, almost in a rush,
of their renovated HGTV bathroom
with a Kohler spray-set shower from the closest Lowes
loosely bundled up
on their Tom Hillbright towel from the newly open Marshalls
waiting
     to smell
  to hear
       to see
 to touch
once more their missing son
Father & mother holding hands dripping more than one type of old-classified liquid

Back to the Future

We might as well hang guns on the ears,
carry them around the wrists and ankles
(instead of on purses, wallets,
shoes, clothes, belts, hats and pockets).
Bead after bead on necklaces
holding an automatic bullet
ready for a touch easier & faster
than a spit of saliva, of *quenepa, caimito* or *parcha* seeds,
a mosquito, a worm, very hot tea, cocoa or coffee,
polluted water, pesticide, rat or cockroach poison.

Much less than a spider step, a flash thought—
Our very own before we can even imagine it.

Up to the Head

i obviously detest, i can't help it,
those who easily show off crossed feet up
(especially barefoot with long, uneven toenails)
against the dusty or shiny dashboard
or the side-front window regardless of the risk
of the sun's revelations, its ultra-violet rays,
the feet tapping, more so a few chosen toes,
to the rhythm of high-volume radio waves,
a Hawaiian plastic doll,
an FSU Seminole garnet & gold necklace
or whatever distraction
hangs on the rear mirror,
same as inside their swollen chests
as if automatically deserving
all patting, rubbing, and *muchimuchi* kissing.

I guess they haven't taken the lead
not completely not yet,
cause I want to believe like rational human being
I detest the feet more than their brains
apparent in the car's color paint,
the horn's sound, the bumper stickers, the middle finger.

Jesus as always, appears way ahead. He doesn't care if feet are up
inside the cars of members of his driving Daytona church,
any Sunday morning in hot & humid Florida.

The Ways of the Feet

We come as we go.

Who fractures his ankle
may be led to *nuevas razones* (a new way of thinking).
Beginning with the foot type
plano or *arqueado*, flat or arched.
Ridículo is having watched that Univision's commercial
of a medicine for the *pie de atleta*.
People showing right in front of a Miami camera,
between their toes their infected area.
"¿En que vamos a parar?," My aunt almost cried, her face a prune.
In good Spanish same to ask, where will we "stand up,"
as in "stand up" or "arrive" or "stop"?
But they aren't the same words.
You tell me once again as if I don't know.
I tell you I haven't forgotten. I don't ignore
like those who fracture their ankle before fracturing their femur.
Under one sole skin they show up
in front of any foot to compare/compete?
Statements turning into questions
worthy of being written down in print or in cursive
ready for the half-closed half-enclosed leather shoe:
A surprising little piece of ancestral rock
to remind each & every one of us
to keep looking for deeper questions, uncomfortable answers,
like anyone who fractures the same ankle
two or three times, in more than one area.
There are more challenges
with almost four feet and crutches,
a cast that can be recoated. Keep horizontal.
A personal signature over the other.
Those who heal, they heal because they need it or not.
Like those who are for a long and good walk.

But then it goes back to the feet,
the earth, *la tierra*, because she herself is
the feet & the rotating surface with subterranean tectonic plates,
sinkholes, volcanoes
that continue to fracture, to heal, or not really.

Protagonism

When we remove a flower from its designated garden
We keep coming with the fragrance and its drooling absence
The fragrance is carried by the common air
We smell as in we aren't the main most unique aromatic subject
Not even as accumulated petals, leaves
There's this trunk in the middle of the jungle, its feet, our feet?
This blur of middleness that better exists
A surmised distance from the top, the bottom
Oh such a bottom! Its new shapeless identity, "Beyond"
Any unimaginable foot over any unimaginable dirt platform

Over Imposed

Never seen
feet being beaten,
apart from a pair on screen
South Korean guests
with a stick
going after the soles
of their friend,
their relative:
The new groom, his bride
Laugh after laugh

Never seen shackles
on ordinary feet
I've seen them on
a padded surface
behind FAMU Black Archives' glass,
the AC blasting,
windows sealed shut
Who still uses a stick
to laugh?
Who's still trapped by shackles,
rusty or shiny, a slave, adult or child?
On pages from an oozing trunk,
through the same human blood
covered by the same sun?

We're living this very second
Nobody can stop us
Not even the many dead
I see prisoners
with their name tag
dressed up in infinite stripes
black & white
under the rain
picking up trash on Crawfordville Highway.
No back or front side of the screen or glass

Nonsynonymous

[S]ome say that the pomegranate was the real apple of Eve... –Janette Winterson.

Feet don't have to parallel, to perfectly match.
Trying to match them, a tiresome (pronounced in French) endeavor.
Although it could justify such benevolent disturbance,
like many others that exist incrementally in life
(some picking while waiting in line), like when:

clutching a long branch coming closer to the right eye interrupting
the unrolled fainted-blue sky,

smelling the dirty second-hand pants, the right leg with paint spots
(already planning their next wash),

looking at the not so subtle lines on the worn-out sidewalk,

        while hearing over the cracked uneven cement the nail
that's gradually come through the sole of the left green boot,

        while eating half of a Greek goddess' pomegranate.

EVOLUTION

Better to conquer yourself than others –Gautama Buddha

In camouflage we get trapped
between such capable legs,
squeezed like a stretching ball, white, black or purple.
Lourdes, *como siempre* walks as if nothing else, nothing at all.
She hears singing, Roy Brown's "Sal a caminar" (Go Head and Walk)—
A piece of Berber fabric inside its own rug.

There's one leg next to the other on the stage, puppetlike
resting on the lap of Ramdas Padhye,
as if one of the best & smartest, trusted Hindu gods.
There's bowing in front of a packed multicultural London.

Now they hang from clotheslines, the distracted; the lazy legs?
save their clang like the bells on the cows of the Naath.
Could it be that in our early stages
we forget the wires like we later forget our real names?

There are the second, the ultimate legs.
There are the first, the literal of bone & flesh
coming out of Africa since 70, 000 years ago.
Even Lourdes, "You tell me once more from such a loose imagination:
A turtle riding a racing horse, crabs flying with egrets' wings
gracefully over the Gulf of Mexico.
Hands covering the bottom, feet stitching beyond the top."
In reproductive magnetic circles?

Of Legs & Gods (or The Bloody Prayer with Question Marks)

Growing up and reading from the Bible, "And even the very hairs of your head are all numbered." (NIV) Matthew 10:30, I could not help but imagine my body covered by little legs instead of hair. To me this meant more that God checks on us, every step we take, especially bad, in order to correct us in whatever way necessary, than that God knows all our needs and is ready to supply each one of them.

Crawling, hanging no more,
walking on our feet
have trapped us in evolving destiny.
Our hands freer to gather, hunt, cook,
eat something like *patitas*, pigs' legs.
On my last trip back home to Puerto Rico
I requested Mami to cook them not just for me.
I've given up red meat, but I couldn't pass *patitas* (with chickpeas):
To lick my fingers.
I'd first started to refuse *lechón* during that time in my life
when Papi raised pigs to sell especially during *la Navidad*
(no pigs, no Christmas).
Several times on a Saturday morning
ready to cry, heart pumping faster than usual,
hands & fingers stirring the air
glimpsing through the window, I heard *mi cochinito*
squealing desperately,
tied up and put on the black Ford truck of Baltazar.
I told my God, myself two, three, four times
itching my throat, my arms, how sorry I was,
that I loved *mi cochinito* very very very much.
Not all pigs are the same, though.
I couldn't eat those I'd helped take care of.
Humans aren't the same as other species.
We eat what we gently walk into,
touch after first seeing it with intrigue, profound appreciation,
even devotion in the jungles, the wild savannas,
at the zoo behind bars and/or glass— buffaloes, monkeys, giraffes...

I remember when teaching an anthropology class
the students' shock after watching in a documentary a group of Jo̸/hoansi men
(could have been women) from the Kalahari Desert killing an adult giraffe
to feed their band of less than sixty members.
Don't we kill chickens, pigs, cows, lambs
in such manners, in such numbers
as if we ought to feed the whole universe at once?
Still on our two feet, our freer hands to touch and grab,
our eyes taking up more of a greater, even if blurry distance.
Flying birds, swimming fish themselves
have tried to convince me I should stop consuming them.
Vegetarianism whispers in my right or left ear *mi nombre y apellidos*
often.
But I get easily hungry for Mami's turkey *en fricasé*,
Hutton shrimp, New Leaf lemon chicken,
Tom's mullet caught in the Gulf of Mexico.
Maybe it has more to do with being able to stand,
to move ahead, way ahead no tail behind, *por supuesto*.
Maybe bipedalismo is *el último responsible*.
We continue as Homo sapiens sapiens
with such unique symbolic thinking, *pensamiento abstracto—*
ideas, reasons/xcuses, gods?:
"Bi & Pe & Dalism" tri-transfigured:
"take & drink & eat"
As we speak/are we eating? In the name of the Father, each other?
And especially of the Lamb of God, are we eating each other?
And of the Spirit.
Amen.

Backward Magic

My grandmother used to say cold to warm is better than warm to cold.

Underneath the surface
There are paths & operations
We don't know of,
Not even walking & walking the various walks.

Except for my uncle and my friend Pedro,
Both who seem to be close with real cold
Against their own warmth,
At times their real heat—
Such magnetic transferring of appetite slowly opening
The vertical heart that's been temporarily out of reach.

Closed Up

Lines on the knuckles
Don't just happen.
They're passed down.

How exactly-exactly
They're passed down
Should tell us less

Than we can handle
Or more than we can imagine
After they've been imitated almost perfectly

Over ceramics and wallpapers,
Traced from underneath the soils,
Perhaps from the Biggest Toes.

Feet Apparitions

There needs no ghost, my lord, come from the grave to tell us this. —Shakespeare

Those hanging from a border cargo train

Ready to become *la raíz* (the root). Nailing it

Like extinct Tsembaga pigs   not many noticing

Those inside an improvised morgue (a refrigerated truck)

Perhaps a beige tag

Tie*d*

Green or ripe to a certain (an alien?) an officially flying mind

With toenails without toenails with a toenail polished by radium or lithium

Ex-iled/In-iled

Those simply sharp, simply flat

Those written plus drawn

Half or fully magic marker/pencil colored

Those a mold of kneeling love   running after   as before

We let them stay for awhile *a lo* Minangkabaou, go like sand, vapor!

 Tic-toc, tic-toc , tic   toc, tic   t   oc

Those untouched by microbes; invisibles?

Those one after the other, up & down (in a portrait of pharaoh or a *conquistador*)

Those the rain dripping from bending windows

Those the magnifying stars many insist on seeing against the black hole

Fourth

And if we close our eyes, do we see the legs(') real kind?

Mortals

They didn't have much trouble
teaching the ape to write poems:
first they strapped him into the chair,
then tied the pencil around his hand
(the paper had already been nailed down).
Then Dr. Bluespire leaned over his shoulder
and whispered into his ear:
"You look like a god sitting there.
Why don't you try writing something?"
—James Tate

I'm sorry for the poems or parts of them
I haven't shared up to this apparently accurate moment.
But listen to me once again:
The second to last gave me the nicest & most extravagant cart ride
then, it left me on the side
of the road in the middle of the gloomy & cold night
tentatively waiting
for the next bright & wholehearted morning.
At the edge of this gripping point,
I don't really know where god's gone.
The next written
        with the feet of the Sahelanthropus—an atheistic antonym?

ALICIA'S DREAMING

Dreams cannot be donated, borrowed or bought, except in Karen Russell's world.

Alicia's single dream to continue to provide more & more full spoons for her acclaimed poetry Playing keys of leaves in two green tonalities coating the sky light-to-dark orange, the grass with tan coated brushes Days began to pedal & pedal to no sleep no dreams no poetry The more she forced herself into such sleeping, the less she could hard-stitch melanin into the quilt of her full young body not even piece by piece, not even slowly & carefully Her mouth overloaded with pale-yellow synthetic feathers, she now dances her legs paralleling the waves of the ocean and from pink to purple rocks, as if they are the world's more than twenty continents She blinks incapable of living asleep or awake this not too black over not too white poem next to its invisible photograph

Inspired by Moca Chen's FSU master thesis film: You Are Dreaming (2011).

Readers of a Kind

A little above the top line
of the black cotton-knit pants
worn by an over two-hundred pound
middle-aged woman

who bends to put food in her old truck
(a bunch of faded stickers almost afloat).
She shows evidence of a thin bikini, of less vs. more cloth,
masking tape, a belt,

the hand, tissue paper; ear plugs?
Do we also talk
with our ears, our nose,
our belly button, our pores; our bottom?

My grandmother once told me,
jar & lid in her tired & shaky hands,
that some holes would be better off
left open, others completely shut.
That it doesn't depend much on how long/
what's inside, but instead what they might attract,

like this commonly covered, uncovered,
light & uneven, odd but apparently qualified enough
p
                      o
               e
       m

The Illustrated Poem (or My Uncle on His Visionary Deceased Father)

He's
been all about
his father, now a perennial shadow
on a piece of paper with a quite rectangular shape
Some letters seemingly wasted. A necklace that breaks and many of
its beads
(not pearls)
roll down, although uncontaminated after going over a puddle of
five-day urine.
There's still
some tracing paper left now in the form of a squished-down circle.
Anyone gladly welcomed
yet without
their amputa-
tion
s.

All of Us at Some Criss-Cross

I could stomp my feet in flat anger,
Jump out of effervescent joy.

Stomp, stomp ... jump, jump ...
Stomp/Jump-Anger　　　　Joy
Split as my two legs in my recent trip to Hong Kong;
Its rich penthouses, its poor rooftops,

Stenciled in a large piece of heavy-style origami paper
Well sustained at either side, I learned, by bamboo poles,
Pointing at the distinguishable main entrance.
There are two main human *prototipos*, as in simple right & wrong.

Under one of a kind thick magnolia,
I stand for a short while, but I'm definitely not the only *turista*
Who slouches first to try to rest.
Some of us go ahead and bend our hips & legs,
Our knees start such an illusion game, quite strategic
Of "completely" crossing our legs for some audience, including ourselves.
We cross them, our legs.
We cross them at our own pace.
And we cross them
& cross them with the help of our arms,
Our hands & fingers,
Our heads like eager poets.

Who Cares for First When There's Second (A Poem: A Reincarnation)

My heart jumps
to the kick inside my womb.
A simple ordinary reaction?
An evolutionary tale of an anticipated ripple?
These days of glimmering sun over the Suwannee River,
far removed from the stagnant ponds
of impatience and incompleteness,
what's now before its then?
Who's to be first, seventh, eleventh?
We've come to terms as if empty-handed
with the "who cares" or "caring too much" mind-set
conscious/unconsciously.
Snakes of different colors flying, hens
as a root system. We pin down with another kick
underground shifting New York cables
until which billboard's baby is next.

Such a Nail

that does not need the skin to retract to appear to be growing, even after death

Winged

I've come so far
    a new graphic persona
        going after the coolest, softest soil
    filtered through an extensive promising list
of un-easy-to-reach, vaulting alternatives
        Enough years have passed of fewer fuzzes;
a little old, a little opaque

I've made a tacky turn around
    to a cooler soil, surely not the coolest nor the softest—
        A percentage actually from my old tropical bench
with over-bars
    & underneath the columns of flying choices,
    trying to make *la diferencia*—
    plenty of premature artistic captions,
        now my accumulated rock-climbing claws' designs

Representative Dancer

For the many J. S.

With the automatic feet of a ballerina since he for long danced the ballet, it seemed clear he was mostly committed to somewhere outside the window, *ay, tan lindo* landscape. Like my uncle Lemuel inside his on-sale casket, a sign apparently read, "To be seen only from the waist up in the nicest second-hand tuxedo." Somewhere a bar code instead of a tattoo of *la cruz de Cristo*; the barcode like the mark of TV *Roots'* slaves, the same day he should have been liberated from the rampant fury of the smart devil.

Tammie & I saw the dancer one night, our heads on our pillows stuffed with soft feathers galloping fast enough over glittering tall flowers before succumbing to the enormous background decorated with childish heart-shaped construction paper.

A mere coincidence?

And it wasn't simply because he could've passed as a teenage Buddhist monk, the Mexican *angelito negro*.   More than Tammie & I, he'd learned to carry at each side of his back, even while doing his most applauded dance, an imperfect record sticker-to-your-skin   with the kind of edges that cut profusely, emanating blood, easily leading to a deadly infection;   pain in the meantime, of course, to which to add   a half-working compass for the purpose of overall exaggerated prevention-a detour from the risk of sincere, authentic levitation. Pro-indexical?

Tammie & I could swear having noticed him coming out quite poignantly, a drizzled morning to be exact   when we seriously speculated following the most realistic script   about all of his waist down, while we touched with one hand making almost a fist the bottom of the dining table,   at the same time we touched with the other,   fingers quite separated,   our semi-heavy hearts.

For some time Tammie & I fell into the plot of his feet already becoming exhumed wreckage before a backward curing amputation.

We kept hearing the claims sometimes screamed, sometimes almost silently,   while digitally restated,   of those who believe to know it all   as if they've been the tissues & bones of all "The Feet of the World,"   as if of the head simultaneously.   Trying to do everything in their hand, they continue to force the feet to the most gigantic & detached pillars,   pillars able to support a fearful & unstable modern world,
el mismísimo universo   keeping it in the natural order, in control under the most superb god.

Behind small & big screens glued to big walls, Tammie & I saw lines and more lines of them holding   signs,   a few even siding all of a sudden with the mothers of poor Chicago *negros*, billboards of neon clarification about the fault of conspiring communist demons.   But there's   tru-
th   for you; for most, for all?

In the aftermath, Tammie & I could've asked the dancer permission   to open the lower second   door   to also see him waist down   in his most practiced medley dance,   his legs scissors   cutting the unrestrained air   making new tree designs, including fruits & flowers smelling pleasantly and primordial.   In the fungi of our minds?

Tammie & I finally   saw   his full body; one of the greatest experimental   attempts
             at loving
             as much & as many as possible.
             Our feet unlike the
         dancer's,   no-bullets-no-holes/Our
unveiled casket
             over high tide   almost
                 f

                                                         t
                             lo   a

         a

MINIATURE ARTS

Dedicated to at least two returnees from the Peace Corps.

two students prayed intensely before their awaited mission trip to Liberia that this beautiful land finally gets decorously tied to its original feet, immediately they found themselves incapable of guaranteeing perfect-future hints like those of a children's hunting game in a museum of prehistory, did their job gracefully massaging molding filling the land but mostly the feet & the rest of the feet's bodies, including the heads, the dead ones, while daring to assign their present commensurate moment to a bodiless eternity until that day at the "well-done" table which they could only stretch so far as such accumulative indication of how their duet mural painting could be prevented from peeling off, such a compacted box delivered to their house in need of painting finally unpacked—tiny brushes covered by micro toenail clippings and invisible dust

[Palimpsest]

Layer I
Don't forget that some of us started shaving our legs
with or without our fathers' Gillette to look better,
a few quitting earlier than expected.
I think of Glenda who went through the back & forth labyrinth
until she stopped after seeing *La Milagrosa* at a world folk festival,
a wave showing off the reunion of sand and rocks at the bottom,
beds of spices & herbs, clusters of different types of inviting
wildflowers.

Layer II
Photograph so that things can stay beautifully intact?
Ask Rex, David, Montesa, Era, Steve, Bob, Floyd, Paco, Augusto,
Katie, Erica, little Jonah.
Without an updated digital camera with the perfect lenses, in
addition to:
temples of debt & waste,
blankets of thirst & hunger,
the shortage of clean air, the absence of accentuating rain.

Layer IIb
I spent one lethargic day after the other
voiceless, fragile-sick,
flipping through the photo album pages.
I searched while stitching over the album's cover
one color escorting the other,
trying to uncover, to keep, to fix, expecting equinoctial things to
magically transfer.
Instead I was dragged to a vaulted, indifferent clear surface,
then forced inside a hoarder's house, barking more & more at the
indoors
while being completely torn apart.

Layer III
Can you or I recall when you or I were born,
immediately wrapped in cute pity, high-pitched joy?
Some say yes if you & I stop
acting as if we never came out of the divinely mysterious.

Layer IV
We've inherited the sticky worm scene of fear
after a second sliding door coated with more than the image of those
who've killed,
those who can easily kill, many without a gun to merely over-exist
making it look futile, impossible hand-brushing with syrup,

any brush-plastering with gum that once belonged
to innocent South American acacia trees.

Surface V or VI
Shouldn't we pause, go back to the source,
the spring, the ever-present love traversed by Ultimate Hope?
We might know what it can fully and further develop into,
what it can ultimately mean
for instance, a hugging mountain top
even after it's been forcefully obliterated,
a kissing moonlight after the eloquent sun
vanishing away.
Perhaps we should keep running like water in the sink
exchanging dreams as customary
not only to and for ourselves.
Put on a band-aid,
yes, our sustained intentions following the doorway:
"One step at a time," add to the fourth or fifth potency
pieces of the classical noble, the ever-present celestial.

Top Surface VIIIA
Like his mother Glenda, Bob finally stopped
trying to simply remove, preserve or cover up
the white hair on his head, his eyebrows, his ears, his nose,

and between his legs, drawing more than once
over second-coated canvas, the kind of stars
anyone can easily confuse it with reverential lily pads.
He's been reading lately more with the eyes of the heart his folded &
unfolded sheets of paper, his clanging coins, his reversible mirrors,
his second-hand printed clothes,
his wrinkled skin,
his temporary walk unawaitin'.

Comortales

But why did the queen specifically state that it was necessary to efface the tattooing on skin of her dead consort in order to assure his place in paradise? For all the effort and inventiveness that the Marquesans lavished on the art of tattoo, they explicitly believed that their gods were not tattooed.
From "Closure and Multiplication: An Essay on Polynesian Cosmology and Ritual," by Alfred Gell.

In simple calm & fresh,
palm trees hang as wet as vernacular shells.
A tattoo of the exact color of the skin on my unshaved leg
reads: "Peace long term."

This time quite vividly my soul
rests in a different tourist *destino*—
The small island slowly sinking,
still the risk that's worth.

I'm quiet after all,
immersed in the mammoth beauty of the placid coast
that welcomes each one of us,
completely naked, half completely clothed.
Tattooed, invisibly or not.

Art Unparalleled

His hands used the railing
Not all of it, not at once
The top, the horizontal
Cannot hold itself
Without the vertical
He cuddling,
Adding to each bar,
Each hand, each foot,
Each-bar-each-foot-each bar.
Not caring for rustiness
For half-security

Five years later
Elizabeth's   doctor's visits no more

Her husband   stacks of metal & glass in his front & back
yards
Predominently diagonal

gRown in tranSlation

To Yoko from Mission San Luis in Tallahassee.

started to read while hunching as i normally do
the translation of an anthology of Japanese poetry (given as a gift)
got caught up in one of the poems' calligraphies
the calligraphies as if about to frame the poem all around
even if the calligraphies end up framing only one side
even if the original poem and its calligraphy impossible to under-
stand
I'm a body lifting up its eyes
(Even if hard to believe)
A stem each and every one
of its
pe
tals
花

Doubled out

I was recently reminded
like a little child, history's also about flags
that were once thought of, once designed.
My eighty-nine-year-old friend Isaura
surprisingly believes feet are flags
(Not the other way around). I had to ask:
"Two flags per individual?"
Julia de Burgos wrote
verses to her other, her second(ary?) self.
Benedict Anderson theorized nations are imagined communities
(*razas*, like races!). Flags are real, *reales*.
You can touch them
if they're high and if you're tall,
if they're low, folded or not.
Feet aren't the same, though.
When Filipín was little
he insisted on tracing his own feet,
the feet of his family, friends, anyone who would let him.
He would be so careful, especially with delicate, shaky feet, going between
the smallest toes, and around the nails covered or not with socks or pantyhose.
Every now & then
around a roller skate, prosthesis, even crutches or cane.
He enjoyed it a lot when people felt ticklish.
He gave his tracing his final touches
with extra designs, extra colors, simple or extravagant.
Many eyes responded.
He told his father, mother, siblings, friends, acquaintances
tracing feet was his real calling.
His father & mother, his siblings, friends, acquaintances
couldn't stop laughing.
But those, especially those who are, presumably or not, poets,

including parents, mothers, siblings, friends, acquaintances
should welcome such (gestured) desires
because dreams are dreams. Precisely.
Adamaris, now a marine archaeologist,
still remembers the day
of her 10th birthday at Wakulla Springs,
how after closing her eyes for a wish and blowing her candles,
holding hands with Filipín after he'd just traced her feet,
the sand underneath
started to go away with the slightest of currents,
leaving their four feet ready
for such unusual flagging of the wind.

Up to the Rest of the Body

Newton's First Law of Motion: Every object in a state of uniform motion tends to remain in that state of motion unless an external force is applied to it.

One of more legs off the frame.
Those of us who stay behind,
do we live extra,
more than what's necessary or expected?
Outside, inside, from which angle, from which circle?
Do we live *insuficientes*
                from the framed
Paint
                or the framed
Painter?

On Feet and Mathematics

"Believe it or not, I'm walkin' on air..." –Stephen Geyer

I. Stepping on a Rotten Tomato vs. a Living Frog

Death-stuck-under between the toes

Life

        an impromptu current

                that can't postpone

II. With An Order of Operations

        EveninG uP
  G   i   g
        o   n

                      o   d
                      d

III. Totaling Equivalences

      or not

a visit to Jesus

        with a Hmong Secret War survivor

in the same old designed parachute, looking like one bright meteor

INVENTORS

"Ella piensa con las piernas (She thinks with her legs)." A common saying growing up.
For poetry is against gravity —Ai Weiwei

"I stand," says the mind,
Its lips
In an imperfect circle of nerved liquid.
A suspended bucket filled like Jupiter vs. Venus
Any March to April
Against
A handprint
From the telescope with some of the hair my daughter puts ribbons on,
Its neck over shoulders, quite oceanic.
Next
A mirror
From which to be able to see what has been already seen
After turning on the old light bulb
Coated by mtDNA colored beads,
A recreated world
Buttons from inside the small intestines
Painted vulvas, balls
Coated with micro drawings
Of what perhaps
Should not
Exist (because of poor managing & King Greed).
          Our nakedness
In & out an outdoor foamed bathtub
Looking
Outside a nearby wide-open balcony door
To a few stars that many seem to erase even on their knees:

Clusters & clusters of feet
Following
Dancing way off
The continued micro fibered red spotted

                                                                             E

F

                  A   Q U

                                      R

                                                      I

                          B

The Non-Hysterical Girl Who Cried Other Than Wolf

Crowns aren't for the feet!
    Aren't for the feet!
Crowns
           Aren't for the feet!
    Aren't for the feet!
Crowns are not for the feet!
Crowns aren't for the feet!
    They aren't
        For
                The feet!!

Crowns are never (intended) for the feet.
    They're not (absolutely not) for the feet.
Crowns
    Aren't for the feet!
        Really? (blah, blah, blah)
But for the...

Shh!!!
(Playing hide&seek behind a thick bush of *cruz de malta*, its flowers falling over the feet, the flowers so red the feet could burst into more than the molecules of many others.)

GRACE

What shall we say, then? Shall we go on sinning so that grace may increase?
Romans 6:1 (NIV)

...Foot In...Foot Out

Madame Chachachá wrote
And video-taped that famous song
About herself in all her splendor
Washing not only the feet
But also the boots, the long & thick smelly socks
Of more than a million soldiers

You Do the Hokey-Pokey

My two-year old touches
My eyelashes with the tip of her toes

And You Turn Yourself Around. That What Is All About

Butterflies!

Playgrounds

To the feet of the watch that holds our mere grounds.

Chequi Morena 2 (indoor/outdoor)

One of Erin's many questions:
"Mama, can you snap with your toes making the noise?"
(A deep breath of mine, my lips pressing harder than usual)
 "Then you can really make fireflies & more fireflies happen,"
she blurted out before I could properly answer.

—

Hop(e)scotch 1 (outdoor/indoor)

Should hope
lead us
to the edge
of another
lightly numbered square
in blue chalk
or should it bring us
directly
to the center
of its very own,
even with a piece of an uneven, rough rock?

Fifth

I looked for the five legs of the cat
even after all their amputations.
I stumbled after mine's disappearance.
Eleven grew back:

Legs & cats

PREMONITION

Gravity alone doesn't sink us all
into this widespread world
filled with heavy drops, hollow stones.
Like bees we go flower after flower looking to drink

without an idea of their scientific pseudonyms,
not to mention where flowers really come from.
We're surrounded by ripples of mountains, shorelines
that without regret confirm us we are "in"
(not above the sky or right underneath).

We remain cemented with an ease
in our overly tracked earthly traditions,
which we title: *Staying while Staying*
surrounded by waves of airy inscriptions
that perforate certain inhibitions, like exaggerated hugs.
We hold our hands empty of non-extinction,
a selected happy retro or futuristic visions
alluding to the words from the onion skin black book,
as if a newly invented exhibition.

Originals don't waste any time to address "the beyond"
one and again mythologized, narrated, painted and pictured.
Although without any regret,
pain & suffering step on further ahead
in their full endorsing of our persisting search
for "the better or the best" with or without much effort, us noticing
even,
working under the apparently strict command
of leading between flowers
already multi-billion times randomly or not footprinted.

Oracle Moment

The hazy San Juan night is embodied in the rented indoors of plastic lilacs & porcelain dolls. Outdoors sprayed with petulant lights, high pitched horns, dance placebos. An opaque wall dented by a series of male punches absorbed by pale female skin whose name starts with lowercase "e" implying stains, quite sanguine. But this series is one among a larger collection of punches thrown by the same male figure.

Lowercase "e" now stands at the fourth-floor balcony with a ten-foot-high, opened door made of mahogany. Fragile & inept, still laden with readiness, the one who out of necessity has surrendered to a thickly coated desire for a new lease on life with no sexual breadcrumbs falling off the one side table.

As she straddles a rattling rail, "e" notices her eyes passing over her shirt tied in a knot showing her belly button, her toes each with decapitated wings going in opposite directions—a sign of her deterioration due to a convalescent life after all the efforts to stay strapped to such a relation based on letters & postcards, pain & blood, blurry imagination—as if the only life anyone can possibly use to move on & to re-re-start.

She's perfectly on her way from a long-time indiscretion tied with ribbons of mixed colors between positivist fanfare & humble resignation. Anticipation rules an octave lower. Mosquitoes fly around her head, turning her almost instantly into an angelic candidate.

Right before she's ready to jump, she thinks of the possibility that there could be real & better lilacs & dolls. A sudden outpouring. A relatively elongated pause as in a malfunctioning elevator. Her heart strikes, drives her down the stairs like an old car with a flat tire sensing each circling as an apotheosis.

She's now face-to-face with a strange little girl who continues to struggle trying to tie her rotten shoelaces. Eugenia finally assists her as if Yahaira had been waiting all her life for that redemptive moment.

Smoke of the blown out, second to last candle: The shoelaces finally break. Eugene and Yahaira both walk barefoot holding hands, smiling at each other as a car alarm sounds.

WIDER WEB

To be human is to count the present among one's possessions.
—Rae Armantrout from Itself

What once stepped in it leaves,
The beating of echoing hearts
That yesterday habitually beat
We keep going to the ironed past
Almost two-faces, over an iconic straight line,
As if what's behind never rotated with the pulsating earth, the sun, the clouds, the stars
Future means no surrender, no stepping aside
We don't bend. We dig up the feet with or without all the toes,
Place them on out stretch-marked hands,
Lift them up, the old fossil of footmarks, their tip-toeing, microbes,
Perhaps to win the Oscar,
Perhaps to Mars, Jupiter, the hole with a question mark black or white,
Aside from a volcano, a bomb, some fracking, the leftover trees waiting to be cut?
Though we seem to have roots, some with recognizable knees, a few bended,
The intertwined type of roots,
Though only a few compared to those of the mushrooms, rhizomes that keep surviving, themselves reassuring
Under & beyond concrete, machines, polluting gases, droughts, floods
The earth continues to rotate, to tremble
It disentangles as we also uproot, uproot, reproot
El ruido de muerte de siempre, the persistence sound of shapelessness, such loose distance
For as the ongoing hearts & bodies are now concerned,
There's this suspended not so quiet, yet quite intersected
Peaceful moment

What we call we call more to say to walk the walk; I walk, we walk, them/us. Over the space between steps. Under? Above? Dance or walk? Before jumping. limping; Some digging? What do we call it: the space in between: ancestors, pre-re/incarnation? As I walk, she steps off with the ball of the foot like earlier sapiens, or with the heel to which we have adapted (or maladapted?) Stepping in and out, I step and I step. I s-t-e-p. My mind, my brain? Faster in time than in space, with a notorious Kenyan runner? Maribel with her *tic nervioso* moves her tongue in almost perfect coordination the leg up; she closes her mouth, her foot down showing off. Why do we title it this way, *Up & Down or Down&Up*? Silence? To walk for Walk? Over dirt, cement, who knows what other surface: rocks, mud, rug; asphalt, grass, sand. Water/Air? Is the time/space between steps dead? Is it alive? Over red after black & white: born or unborn same exact life?

If Death were a child, would we keep him in our arms?

Transfiguration

Still overdosed of crude reality:
The slaughter of his brother, five of his sheep,
Acham counts hour after hour until he finally goes to sleep.

After a few mornings, a tiny bit
empty of such brutality,
he swallows the flapping silence with the little piece

of the medium-size bread left
on the forced-to-three-leg table of daily insistence.
He trudges slowly
to the office of blistering interrogations, puncturing mistakes.
Dries with half of his fingers any sweat left on his newly triangular face.
Not far from that time to another left,

a few days after, he positions himself
one leg almost right next to the other
in front of such persisting panoramic cascade

nobody has ever seen, smelled, heard, or imagined.
He directs half a cup with both hands,
his chin tilted, to his half-opened mouth

already wet, similar to his legs,
way above his much steadier,
less swollen ankles.

Rain of Feet

They are reputed to do well with lower extremities, but are challenged to provide upper ones, which, because of the nature of the hand, is so much more complicated.
—Greta Uehling, 2015 (about people with prosthetics in war-torn Ukraine)

Therapy of liminality
Lluvia de pies
Space that's neither
Lluvia de pies
Nor. The Gate
Lluvia de pies
Having to choose today, tomorrow
Lluvia de pies
Yesterday
Lluvia de pies
Life goes on
Lluvia de pies
Regardless
Lluvia de pies
Of the rituals, multicolored
Lluvia de pies
Candles
Lluvia de pies
No candles
Lluvia de pies
With, without trees
Lluvia de pies
& lights. There's still
Lluvia de pies
Life
Lluvia de pies
Evaporated
Lluvia de pies
Lluvia de pies
Lluvia de pies
The Ultimate

Lluvia de pies
Healing: The feet, unlike the hands,
Under awaited new drops
Over unexpected puddles
What we're *de cosa de humanos*
To step on the green of the tip of a magnolia leaf
To lay on the white & blue palm of Eternity

To Push Forward, To Go Back

A la memoria de Amado Nuñez.

Your foot remembers like a violinist's hand,
hands & feet both of elements. Perhaps
the feet amid the bustle of wet leaves
preferring one place of permanent settling,
a kind of diminishing/disappearing?

Amado's two legs of cells, concentrated.
One as if ironing the floor, planting seeds.
The other pointing toward an old woman
whose invisible arms are filled with white lilies.

Both legs trained into the game of heavy clouds,
the first now well-suspended letting the air pass by & around.
The second, a bulged metaphor
of *la vida es la vida*—with its tagged price,
"Not being able *to echarse a andar* (let yourself walk)."
The price tag hangs from the untouchable sky,
at first glance such a dragging effort.

After a while on wheels by Lake Okeechobee,
Amado enters a compensating corner of the small city,
goes through its edges not able to avoid pestilent trash.
He holds his breath more than usual,
a new Olympic athlete demonstrating his extraordinary resistance,

surprisingly stops,
savors the delicious mango he ate when nine years old
with his best friend who ended up
near his feet dead at his same age,
after playing baseball with improvised equipment
en el campo de Cuba, their four legs covered by sugar.

Amado dances. Oh he dances to the most awaited *melodía*.
He breathes air

the rain, the most dispersed,
the most (in good Spanish) *su-bli-me*.

Open-ended

Whether indigenous peoples walking with a more efficient J-back rather than an S-back, or the family in Turkey whose adult children walked most of their life on all fours...

They say women apologize and use "for example" too much, meaning more than men.

our feet the clouds
our heads the roots
the center
(the window of the universe?)
a simple like gum-spit dot?
some dare to say even in plastic; there's pause

        a line
(with some zigzags) to the sky
the other line crossing both sides, some parts cut
still, whether from the left from the right the center
line "to below & to..." in the middle
four other centers, open-ended
northeast
northwest
southeast
southwest
forgive me, but we eliminate
and eliminate, and eliminate even if we rotate
the real center (or the fake?)
For example, even when we are sitting, we hug excluding the legs

        everywhere & forever?

The Feet That Breathe

Looking at any point, except the one we stand on
is stretching our moment in infinity.
And what's the line in between?
Isn't it the roots, the dirt, the leaves and petals,
the fruit, the butterfly,
the bird that sings and flies fast, but slowly for the most part,
attached to a small or the big hand, the planets, the stars?

The feet	Los pies
microscopic	microscópicos
from the planets down	de los planetas hacia el suelo
with a name	con un nombre
to hold onto	del cual agarrarse
to carry on	para cargar
like a turtle's shell	como el caparazón de la tortuga
slowly moving ahead.	yendo poco a poco para adelantarse.
Where's the air	¿Dónde está el aire
that breathes itself first,	que se respira el mismo primero
right above, right under	exactamente arriba y abajo
not a foot at a time	no un pie a la vez
but many, all	sino muchos, todos
almost at once?	al mismo instante?
The feet, two, four, many more	Los pies, dos, cuatro, muchos otros
continue microscopically	continúan microscópicos
from the Milky Way up.	de Milky Way hacia arriba.
The Air's here,	El Aire está aquí
well around to stay.	bien alrededor para quedarse.
Already on its way	Ya de camino

       forever wing-opened   para siempre

                                          de-alas-gigantes

Left   Right
                                        (its sole the most worn,
                                        the back-right side)

Acknowledgments

I would like to thank the editors from *The Griot: The Journal of African American Studies*, who published the poems, "The—N—word" and "Over Imposed" (Spring 2017, 36.1, 49-52), included in this collection.

Many thanks to the non-profit organization, Palaver Tree Theater, and its founding members and volunteers from my home town of Crawfordville, for providing a vibrant platform for the arts and community service projects. Thanks to Palaver's director, Herb Donaldson, for his tireless efforts and valuable encouragement.

I am grateful for the camaraderie of poets in the Tallahassee area who support each other and join together as a unified voice for social justice and peace. To the friends from the 621 Poetry Gallery, 100 Thousand Poets for Change, and Big Bend Poets & Writers: Thank you. Thanks also to Poetas Sin Fronteras (Poets Without Borders) for the opportunity to connect with poets worldwide and to bring poetry to local communities.

Love and light to my friends Karen Rose, Nitya Pandey, and Cassie LeJeunesse for their encouragement and editing of my poems. To my poet friends Jonathan Harrington, Jodi Hunt, Phoebe Fillis, Mary Jane Ryals, and especially, Indran Amirthanayagam and Josephine Yu, for being sources of inspiration, for sharing great conversations, and for their commenting on this book.

Sincere thanks to Ruth Thompson, owner and editor of Saddle Road Press, for giving a home to *The Five Legs of the Cat*, my first poetry collection in English. You have given me an enormous gift. To Don Mitchell (another poet anthropologist): I cannot thank you enough for your patience, thoughtful comments, attention to detail and consistency.

To Puerto Rican artist, Andrés Tavárez, thank you for immediately saying yes to sharing your evocative and visionary art for the cover of this book.

Deep gratitude and love to my parents Josué Hernández and Irene Hiraldo for sustaining me in ways that I appreciate more with each passing year and to my brother Josué Hernández for standing by me, making me laugh and for his constant reassurance. Special thanks to my husband Paul Fortier and my daughters Adriana and Erin Fortier for reading early drafts and for honest critique and editing. To them and my son Rafel Fortier: There is nothing that can compare with your love and good humor.

About the Author

Samiri Hernández Hiraldo was born and raised in Puerto Rico. She earned a Ph.D. in anthropology from the University of Michigan and has taught Anthropology, Religion, Women Studies, and Latino/Afro-Latino Studies. She currently teaches these and other subjects at Florida A&M University and conducts research on re-africanization in Puerto Rico and the Puerto Rican diaspora.

Hernández Hiraldo has written articles, chapters, and book reviews on the above topics. In 2006 she published her book, *Black Puerto Rican Identity and Religious Experience* (University Press of Florida 2006; 2014).

In 2012 Hernández Hiraldo was awarded as a finalist on the shortlist of the National Poetry Series' Paz Prize for Poetry competition (in honor of Octavio Paz) for her poetry collection, "Entre borrosas guardarrayas" (Between Blurry Boundaries). Her poems have appeared in *PALARA* (Publication of the Afro-Latin/American Research Association), *Chicana/Latina Studies: The Journal of Mujeres Activas en Letras y Cambio Social*, *The Griot: The Journal of African American Studies*, *The Acentos Review*, *Azahares*, *Latin American Literary Review*, *Latino Book Review*, *Letralia, The Journal of Latina Critical Feminism* and *Revista Innombrable*.

Her collection of poetry, *Al Vapor* (Steamed) was published in August of 2020 by Editorial Calíope in Madrid, Spain, and *Cuando el líquido es sólido* (When the Liquid Is Solid) in January of 2021 by Publicaciones Entre Líneas in Florida, United States.

Hernández Hiraldo also coordinates poetry events as a board member of Palaver Tree Theater, a non-profit community organization serving the Big Bend Area. She shares her poetry with different audiences, including young students. She is a proud participant in the 100 Thousand Poets for Change, Big Bend's Poets & Writers (a chapter of Florida State Poets Association), and Poetas Sin Fronteras (Poets Without Borders).

www.ingramcontent.com/pod-product-compliance
Lightning Source LLC
Chambersburg PA
CBHW031122080526
44587CB00011B/1074